My Boyfriend
IS A
BEAR

My Boyfriend

IS A

BEAR

written by
PAMELA RIBON

illustrated and colored by
CAT FARRIS

♥

lettered by
SAIDA TEMOFONTE

color assists by
**CAITLIN LIKE, GABRIEL FISCHER,
RON CHAN, ALLYSON WILLSEY & JON SIRUNO**

AN ONI PRESS PUBLICATION

designed by **Kate Z. Stone**
edited by **Ari Yarwood** and **Charlie Chu**

♥

Published by Oni Press, Inc.

Joe Nozemack founder & chief financial officer
James Lucas Jones publisher
Charlie Chu v.p. of creative & business development
Brad Rooks director of operations
Rachel Reed marketing manager
Melissa Meszaros publicity manager
Troy Look director of design & production
Hilary Thompson senior graphic designer
Kate Z. Stone junior graphic designer
Angie Knowles digital prepress lead
Ari Yarwood executive editor
Robin Herrera senior editor
Desiree Wilson associate editor
Alissa Sallah administrative assistant
Jung Lee logistics associate

onipress.com
facebook.com/onipress
twitter.com/onipress
onipress.tumblr.com
instagram.com/onipress

pamie.com / @pamelaribon
cattifer.com / @Cattifer

First Edition: April 2018
ISBN 978-1-62010-487-3
eISBN 978-1-62010-488-0
Library of Congress Control Number: 2017952716

PRINTED IN CHINA.

1 2 3 4 5 6 7 8 9 10

For Jason.
You ripped open that "It's It"
and that was it for me.
Grah.

PAMELA RIBON

For Ron.
Thanks for bearing with me.

CAT FARRIS

My Boyfriend

IS A

BEAR

MY NAME IS NORA. I'M 28 YEARS OLD AND I LIVE IN A ONE BEDROOM APARTMENT ON THE EAST SIDE OF LOS ANGELES.

MY BOYFRIEND IS A 500-POUND AMERICAN BLACK BEAR.

ISN'T HE HANDSOME?

HOLLYWOOD

Things broken by the Bear.

BUT HE HAS *NEVER* BROKEN MY HEART.

SOME PEOPLE THINK IT'S STRANGE THAT I DATE A BEAR. THEY SAY THEY'D BE TOO SCARED. WELL, *THAT'S STUPID.*

DID YOU KNOW THAT YOU ARE *180,000* TIMES MORE LIKELY TO BE KILLED BY A *BEE* THAN A *BEAR?*

IT'S TRUE!

BZZZZ

PEOPLE: DON'T DATE BEES!

I'M NOT THE EASIEST PERSON TO LIVE WITH, EITHER.

EVERY REPORT CARD EVER.

COATS I USE THREE DAYS OUT THE YEAR. ('SUP, L.A.?)

...I HAVE A TENDENCY TO HANG ONTO THINGS.

I SOMETIMES CRY FOR HOURS, TOO EASILY.

I HAVE THIS WEIRDO JOB WHERE I BASICALLY LISTEN TO PEOPLE YELL AT ME ALL DAY LONG.

THESE TWO THINGS MAY BE RELATED.

BUT TONIGHT IS DIFFERENT. TONIGHT, I'M TAKING EXTRA LONG TO DO EVERYTHING.

BECAUSE I AM TRYING TO MAKE TIME SLOW DOWN UNTIL IT JUST STOPS.

I FEEL SO SELFISH.

I KNOW THIS ISN'T HIS FAULT.

IT'S NOT MINE, EITHER. BUT IT'S GOING TO CHANGE THINGS.

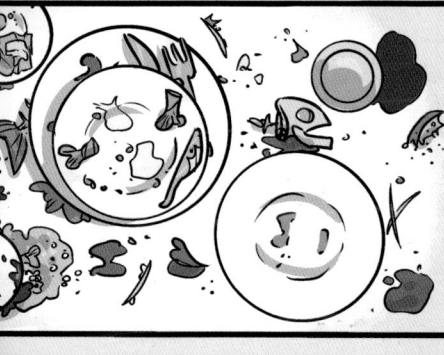

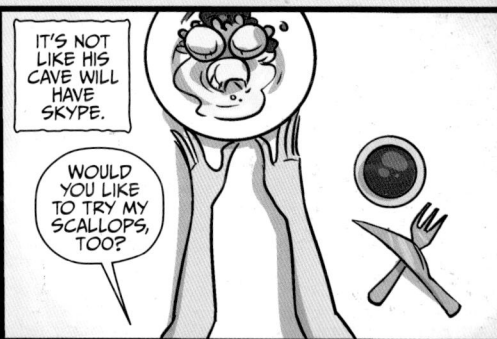

IT'S NOT LIKE HIS CAVE WILL HAVE SKYPE.

WOULD YOU LIKE TO TRY MY SCALLOPS, TOO?

I CAN'T BELIEVE HOW QUICKLY THE TIME HAS GONE.

IT STILL FEELS LIKE WE MET ONLY YESTERDAY.

BACK TO BEN.

THE NATIONAL

WHAT ARE YOU DOING?

SHAPE

...READING?

THAT'S NOT READING!!

GLAMOR

AND
HIS STUPID
FACIAL HAIR
SMELLS LIKE
FOX PEE!

MY BEST FRIENDS ARE DEBRA AND CARLY.

DEBRA: MISERABLY SINGLE. SELF-CONSCIOUS ABOUT HER EARS. WANTS TO GET MARRIED AND HAVE A HUGE FAMILY. WORRIES SHE'LL PICK THE WRONG HUSBAND. WHEN I'M SINGLE, SHE'S LIKE VELCRO.

CARLY: CURRENTLY HAS TWO BOYFRIENDS AND A GIRLFRIEND. ALWAYS SMILING, SUPER-SMART, SMELLS LIKE EXPENSIVE HONEY. MIGHT INVENT THE NEXT IPOD OR SOMETHING. CARLY PARTIES HARD AND LOVES GOING ON TRIPS. SHE'S ALWAYS AT THE CENTER OF SOMETHING FUN. I WISH WE WERE CLOSER.

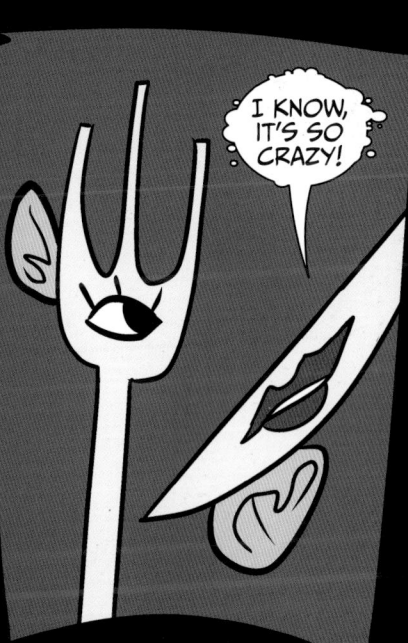

DROP!

YOU ARE A BEAR.

HE
FOUND
ME.

THINGS I LEARNED VERY QUICKLY.

THE BEAR LIKES SPINACH, BLUEBERRIES, AND BEER.

HONEY LAGER

THE BEAR DOES *NOT* LIKE COUSCOUS.

HE FINDS MY DETACHABLE SHOWERHEAD FASCINATING.

I'VE HAD TO BUY DRANO.

SHAKE

SHAKE

SHAKE

THAT ANT PROBLEM IN THE KITCHEN IS FIXED.

12:4

AND SO'S MY BED.

(WE BROKE IT.)

THANK YOU.

GRAH.

HE INSISTS ON TAKING OUT THE TRASH, BUT I KNOW HE JUST WANTS TO GO THROUGH THE BINS.

RING! RING! BEEP! BOOP! RING! BEEP!

I WAS FALLING HARD.

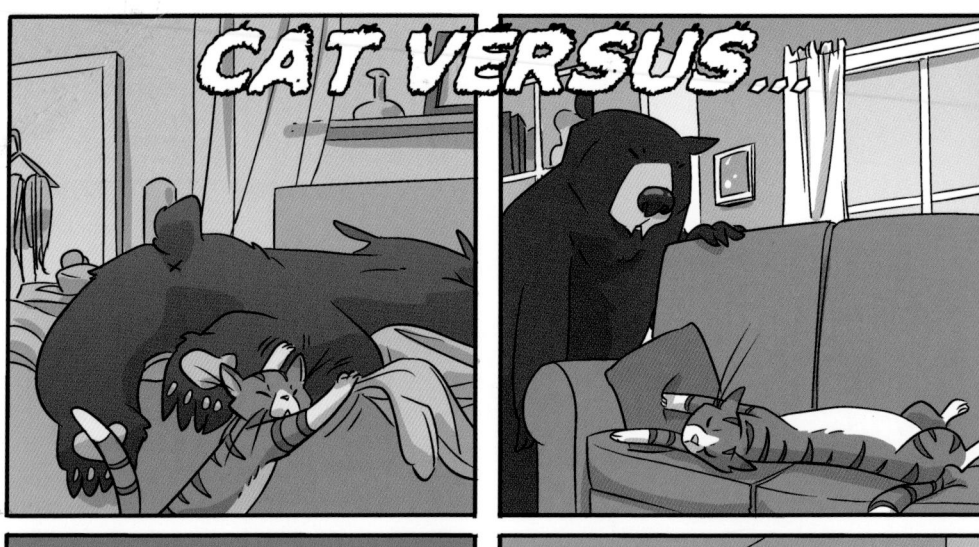

CAT VERSUS...

...*BEAR.*

I KNEW I WAS A GONER WHEN I FOUND MYSELF DOING WHAT I ALWAYS DO WHEN I GO CRAZY OVER SOMEONE.

I LEARN EVERYTHING I CAN ABOUT THEM.

BEARCYCLOPEDIA

~LIVING~
WITH BEARS

BEAR PATTERNS

BEAR WITH ME
A GUIDE FOR COHABITATING WITH BEARS

BEARS! BEARS! BEARS!

BEARS: FRIEND OR FOE?

ALL ABOUT BEARS

YOU ARE AN AMERICAN BLACK BEAR.

YOU ARE NOT A GRIZZLY BEAR.

A GROUP OF BEARS IS CALLED A "SLOTH."

HEH. THAT'S FUNNY. I GET IT.

UH, IT SAYS HERE THAT MALE BEARS ABANDON THEIR CUBS AS SOON AS THEY'RE BORN.

WE'RE GONNA HAVE TO TALK ABOUT SOME OF THESE THINGS.

WE ALSO
LEARNED A VERY
IMPORTANT LESSON...

...EVEN
THOUGH
IT'S FUN...

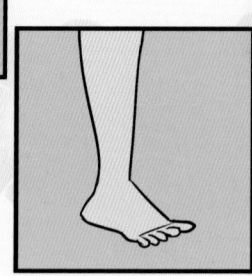

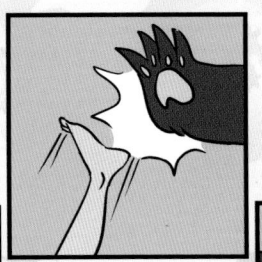

...AND
WE ARE VERY
GOOD AT IT...

...WE HAD
TO STOP
WRESTLING.

OW.

I DIDN'T WANT HIM TO KNOW HOW NERVOUS I WAS.

HI! WE'RE MEETING PEOPLE.

≈WHISPER≈

ARCADE FIRE

SCRICH

SCOOCH

GRAH.

UNFUCKINGBELIEVABLE.

AND THEN...

OH, GOD, IS HE ATTACKING?!

WE DECIDED TO TRY MORE PUBLIC EXCURSIONS.

THE ZOO WAS A BAD IDEA.

SO WAS RUNYON CANYON.

HOLLYWOOD

HOLY SHIT!

RUN, SKYLAR! IT'S A FUCKIN' BEAR, DUDE!

GRRR

RUFF! RUFF! RUFF!

CAT VERSUS BEAR:
PROBLEMS WITH CLAWS

MEW PURR

YEAH, I'D SAY HE'S PRETTY HANDY.

YOU'RE DELUSIONAL. DON'T YOU SEE I'M TRYING TO HELP YOU?

END THIS BEFORE YOU GET HURT!

I'LL CALL YOU LATER, D. I SHOULD GET READY FOR WORK.

YOU'RE PRETTY SWEET, BEAR.

GRAH.

OKAY, SO MY SHITBALLS JOB...

...I WORK AT A CALL CENTER FOR A POP-UP WINDOW SCAM.

SOME PEOPLE CLICK THIS POP-UP WINDOW THINKING THEY WON SOMETHING...

WINNER! ✕

CONGRATS!

...BUT END UP ACCIDENTALLY SIGNING UP FOR A MONTHLY FEE.

NOT *YOU*. YOU DIDN'T SIGN UP FOR THIS. YOU DIDN'T GET FOOLED. BUT THESE PEOPLE DID:

USUALLY NOBODY DISCOVERS THEY'RE AUTOMATICALLY SENDING $14.99 A MONTH TO "INTERNET PARTNERS CLUB," BUT SOMETIMES THEY DO, OR A LOVED ONE DISCOVERS IT WHILE PAYING THE BILLS.

THERE'S A PHONE NUMBER IN THE FINE PRINT TO CALL, AND WHEN THEY CALL IT, SOMETIMES THEY GET *ME*.

YELLING *YELLING*

CURSING

I CAN'T BLAME THEM FOR BEING MAD.

SOMEONE CALLED ME A "SHIT FUCKER" THE OTHER DAY. THAT WAS UNIQUE.

YELLING YELLING

SCREECHING *HUFFING*

Bambi
Ben
Betty

C

home
(310) 555-7823
phone (found in email)
(310) 555-7823
Face Time

Delete Contact

Cancel

GRAH.

BEAR!

GRAH.

⋅GIGGLE⋅
OKAY, LET'S GO!
⋅GIGGLE⋅

GRAH!

(MATING SEASON WAS FUN.)

(SO WAS HALLOWEEN.)

RATTLE

CLINK

NORA, THIS IS NO WAY TO LIVE.

IF I'D KNOWN I'D BE DRAGGING A BEAR TODAY, I MIGHT HAVE WORN DIFFERENT SHOES.

NNNH!

UGH. FORGET IT. WE'LL NEVER MOVE HIM.

THIS IS ALL CARLY'S FAULT.

MMM. IF YOU SAY SO.

IS HE GETTING BIGGER?

I THINK SO.

RAAAHHHHHHH

♪♫ OH, THE WEATHER OUTSIDE IS FRIGHTFUL! ♫♪

♫ BUT THE FIRE IS SO DELIGHTFUL-- ♫

GRAH!

MMF! IT'S SNOW, BEAR! IT'S SNOWING! ISN'T IT GREAT? ARE YOU SURPRISED? DID IT SCARE YOU? I'M SORRY!

HE PULLED BACK TO LOOK AT ME AND I REALIZED: HE WASN'T SCARED. HE WAS SAD.

BECAUSE SNOW AND SCARVES AND THE HOLIDAYS MEANS: HIBERNATION IS COMING.

THE BEAR WAS EXTRA SWEET FOR A WHILE AFTER THAT, AS WE PRETENDED TO COMPLETELY IGNORE THE TICKING CLOCK.

EXTRA FOOT RUBS.

SWIVEL

SWISH

THE BEAR LEARNED HOW TO MAKE POPCORN ON THE STOVE.

WE WATCHED ALL OF DOWNTON ABBEY IN BED.

THAT'S MISTER BATES.

WE FOUND *THE BEST* SUSHI RESTAURANT WHERE THEY ABSOLUTELY *LOVE* THE BEAR.

IRASSHAIMASE!

WHEN IT CAME TO THINKING ABOUT DECEMBER, I WAS LIKE THIS:

LA LA LA LALALALA LA LA LA LA LA LA LA...

--WHICH I ALTERNATED WITH FITS OF *THIS.*

94

MY JOB WAS BECOMING A SHIT PILE, TOO.

HEY, DID YOU SEE THERE'S A NEW SCHEDULE?

THEY CHANGED MY HOURS! HOW CAN THEY JUST *DO* THAT?

BECAUSE THEY WANT US TO QUIT. THIS PLACE IS GOING DOWN THE SHITTER. I HEAR THEY'RE GETTING SUED. I'M NOT QUITTING. I'M MILKING THIS PLACE FOR EVERY LAST PENNY.

HEFTY BEAR

DID I TELL YOU I GOT RID OF MY TELEVISION? BEST DECISION I EVER MADE.

DECEMBER

HEE HEE! I LOVE THEM.

SAY CHEESE... BURGER!

HEY, BEAR?

GRAH.

THE WEATHER'S STAYED PRETTY WARM.

LOOKS LIKE WE MIGHT HAVE A REALLY HOT CHRISTMAS. LIKE, A SUMMERTIME SITUATION.

I MEAN... YOU KNOW... MAYBE...

≥SOB≥

98

WASN'T THAT A *LOVELY* DINNER? A *LONG, QUIET NIGHT* WITH JUST THE TWO OF US! RIGHT, BEAR?

GRAH.

WHERE HAVE YOU BEEN HIDING YOURSELF, NORA-BORA? IF IT WEREN'T FOR FACEBOOK, I'D HAVE THOUGHT YOU'D DIED!

I'M TWENTY-EIGHT WEEKS. I *LOVE* BEING PREGNANT. YOU THINK YOU'LL BECOME A MOMMY SOON?

UM...

I BOOKED A COMMERCIAL THAT'S SUPPOSED TO RUN DURING THE SUPER BOWL, SO THAT'S AWESOME.

I SAW YOUR PARENTS ARE HERE. THAT'S *HILARIOUS.*

WE'VE BEEN READING JOSÉ SARAMAGO? *DEATH AT INTERVALS?* HAVE YOU READ IT?

YOU *HAVE* TO READ IT. IT'S AMAZING. ALL HIS STUFF'S *AMAZING.* YOU SHOULD *TOTALLY* BE READING HIM. YOU'LL *LOVE* IT.

CHEERS, B-DAY GIRL. HAVING FUN?

I GUESS SO. I HAVEN'T SEEN MOST OF THESE PEOPLE IN A WHILE.

ACTUALLY, A LOT OF THESE PEOPLE ARE *YOUR* FRIENDS.

WHATEVER.

WHERE IS THE BEAR?

WITH CARLY IN THE LIVING ROOM. HE'S FINE.

YOU GUYS HAVING FUN?

OH, YEAH. *THIS* GUY. THIS GUY'S THE BEST! I LOVE THIS BEAR. MARRY HIM, NORA.

OKAY, HAVE FUN, YOU TWO. BUT LET MODERATION BE YOUR GUIDE.

KISS

WHERE ARE YOUR BOARD GAMES?

WHAT AM I LOOKING AT HERE?

THE BEAR BUILT THIS FOR NUTSO SO HE DOESN'T GET STEPPED ON.

HERE IN THE KITCHEN, WE CALL IT THE "CATSKILLS." WANNA SEE "CAT-MANDU"?

YES.

WHEN'S THE LAST TIME YOU GOT AN OIL CHANGE?

I KNOW, DAD. I KNOW. I'LL LOOK INTO IT.

NO, YOU'RE SO WRONG, DUDE.

EXCUSE ME, DAD...

YEAH, IT'S A PRETTY COMMON MISTAKE PEOPLE MAKE, BUT ACTUALLY--

EXCUSE ME.

OH, HEY, HAPPY BIRTHDAY!

EXCUSE ME.

THANKS, EXCUSE ME...

WHAT ARE YOU DOING OUT HERE?

BEN'S HERE.

YEAH. I INVITED HIM.

WHY WOULD YOU DO THAT?

I THOUGHT YOU GUYS WERE FRIENDS.

YOU SAID I SHOULD NEVER SPEAK TO HIM AGAIN!

I SAY ALL KINDS OF THINGS.

WHY IS THE BEAR SUCH A PROBLEM FOR YOU? I DON'T GET IT.

LOOK AT HIM.

GO, BEAR!

HA HA HA!

GO, BEAR!

U OF STATE

ARCADE FIRE

OH, MY GOD! HAHA!

WHOA!

SO? HE'S FUN. PEOPLE LIKE HIM.

HE'S A PARLOR TRICK. A CIRCUS FREAK. *THAT'S* WHERE YOU TWO BELONG. THE CIRCUS.

YOU CAN'T HAVE KIDS. YOU COULDN'T EVEN ADOPT. WHO'D LET A BEAR HAVE CHILDREN?

HAS HE EVEN TOLD YOU THAT HE LOVES YOU? NO, BECAUSE HE *CAN'T.* AND HE NEVER *WILL.*

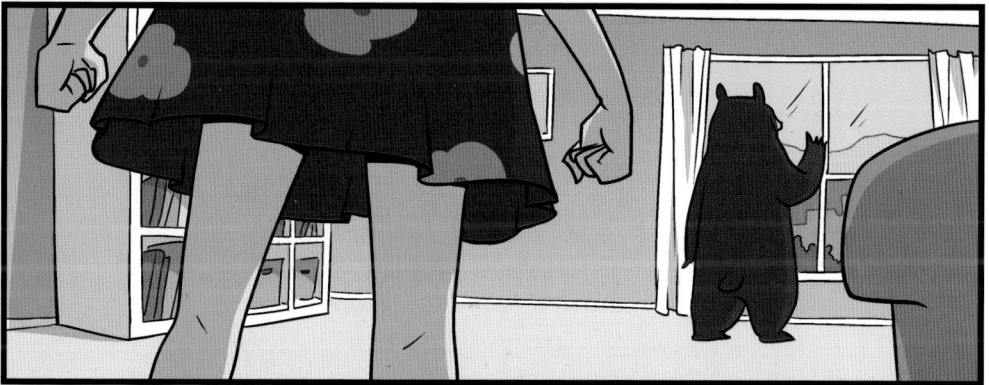

WHEN I WOKE UP
THE NEXT MORNING,
NUTSO WAS GONE.
SO WAS THE BEAR.

HE HAD TAKEN HIM
AWAY BEFORE I
HAD TO SEE MY CAT'S
LIFELESS BODY.

NEITHER OF
US SLEPT WELL
THAT NIGHT.

HE PULLED ME CLOSE INTO
HIS HOT FUR AND I FELT
HIS HEART BEATING.
FAST NOW. WITH ME, NOW.

I WISHED ON ALL MY WISHES
THAT I COULD FALL ASLEEP
RIGHT THEN AND STAY THAT WAY
UNTIL HE CAME BACK TO ME.

I WAS SO JEALOUS. HE
DIDN'T HAVE TO LIVE THROUGH
THE NEXT FEW MONTHS.

HE DIDN'T HAVE TO WAIT.
HE WOULD CLOSE HIS EYES
AND THEN IT'D BE OVER.

IN THE MORNING, I FIXED HIM EVERYTHING IN MY FRIDGE.

OKAY, YOU READY?

GRAH.

IT WAS SORT OF WEIRD, HOW HE DIDN'T NEED A SUITCASE.

IT WAS THE QUIETEST WALK WE'D EVER TAKEN.

DON'T FORGET ME.

2AM 3AM 4AM 5AM

STUFF

GÜRME COFFEE

FOLD FOLD FOLD

GÜRME

HONEY

TUCK

SNIFF

14

SCRITCH SCRITCH

I TRIED TO FILL THE BEAR-SHAPED HOLE IN MY LIFE WITH A BIT OF MY OLD LIFE.

I STARTED WORKING ON A NEW PATTERN.

I VISITED MY PARENTS.

I THINK IT'S BETTER THIS WAY.

STATE U

MOM... PLEASE DON'T.

I WAS ACTUALLY GRATEFUL FOR MY BULLSHIT JOB, BECAUSE IT TOOK UP SO MUCH TIME.

PFF!

HUFF!

LEFT! RIGHT! GO! GO!

I GOT BACK INTO MY WORKOUT ROUTINE.

I HAD DINNER WITH CARLY, WHO ONLY TALKED ABOUT DEBRA.

SHE REALLY MISSES YOU. YOU SHOULD CALL HER.

I TRIED. I REALLY DID. BUT IT ALL FELT EMPTY.

THAT'S THE BIG DIPPER, PART OF URSA MAJOR. WHO KNOWS WHAT THAT MEANS?

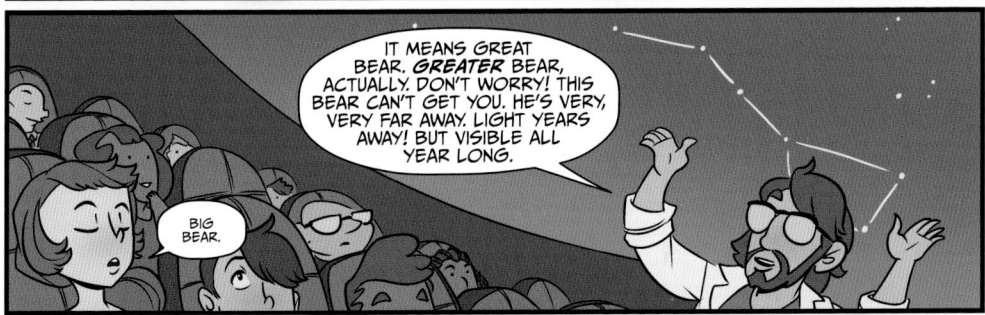

IT MEANS GREAT BEAR. *GREATER* BEAR, ACTUALLY. DON'T WORRY! THIS BEAR CAN'T GET YOU. HE'S VERY, VERY FAR AWAY. LIGHT YEARS AWAY! BUT VISIBLE ALL YEAR LONG.

BIG BEAR.

FIND SOMEONE NICE AND NORMAL. GET MARRIED. MAKE GRANDBABIES.

SINCE WHEN DO YOU WANT GRANDBABIES?

YOUR FATHER AND I WILL BE DEAD EVENTUALLY. YOU MIGHT WANT TO REMEMBER THAT.

MOM! THE BEAR AND I DIDN'T BREAK UP. WE'RE STILL TOGETHER.

YOU'RE GOING TO GO THROUGH THIS EVERY YEAR, LIVING HALF A LIFE?

I DON'T KNOW-- MAYBE!

YOU SHOULD FIND SOMEONE BETTER-SUITED FOR YOU. MY KNITTING CLUB AGREES.

WELL, I DO TAKE MOST OF MY LIFE ADVICE FROM YOUR KNITTING CLUB.

YOU'RE TOO SMART NOT TO KNOW YOU'RE IN A BAD SITUATION. FIX IT.

DING DONG

HI, NORA! COME ON IN! MERRY CHRISTMAS! IS THAT YOUR GIFT? YAY!

JUST PUT IT UNDER THE TREE.

HOLIDAYS!

NO, I HAVEN'T SEEN THAT MOVIE YET.

YOU *HAVE* TO SEE IT.

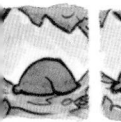
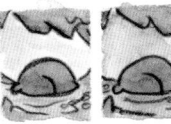

FOURTEEN NINETY-NINE CHARGED TO MY VISA BILL, AND **BEFORE** YOU TELL ME TO CALL THEM, I **DID**, WHICH IS HOW I KNOW YOU **ASSHOLES** HAVE BEEN CHARGING ME FOURTEEN NINETY-NINE EVERY **MONTH** FOR A **YEAR!**

HOW DO YOU PEOPLE **LIVE** WITH YOURSELVES?!

YOU SHOULD BE IN **JAIL!** I HAVE HALF A MIND TO--

WHAT IF DEBRA WAS, IN THE TINIEST WAY, JUST A LITTLE BIT RIGHT? WE NEVER TALKED ABOUT HIS LIFE IN THE CAVE.

WHAT IF HE HAD A BEAR GIRLFRIEND BEFORE HE MET ME? BEFORE HE HAD TO FLEE THE FIRES?

CLICK

COME ON IN, NORA! JUST PUT THE WINE ON THE TABLE.

NO, I HAVEN'T STARTED IT YET.

I *JUST* FINISHED IT. IT'S AMAZING. YOU *HAVE* TO READ IT.

HAPPY NEW YEARS

I WENT TO SEE HIM.

THE BEAR. I WENT TO HIS CAVE. YOU WERE WRONG.

YOU KNOW, PEOPLE ACT LIKE EVERY RELATIONSHIP CAN WORK IF YOU JUST WANT IT TO. LIKE LOVE IS THIS TINKERBELL THING THAT ONLY DIES WHEN YOU AREN'T CLAPPING HARD ENOUGH.

IF THAT WERE TRUE, I'D STILL BE WITH ROBERT.

I LOVED HIM MORE THAN THAT FAIRY BITCH LOVED HER WINGS.

SIX YEARS OF MY LIFE.

I KNOW YOU DID. *DO.*

GODDAMMIT, I HATE MY OWN FEELINGS. PLEASE DON'T LOOK AT ME.

I STILL LOVE YOU, DEBRA.

THE BEAR WAS NEVER TOO FAR AWAY.

HE TOOK UP ALL THIS SPACE IN HERE.

BUT DEAR, I DON'T UNDERSTAND HOW MY MONEY CAN BE **INSIDE** A COMPUTER AND NOT MY BANK. HOW DID THE INTERNET GET THE CARD, DEAR? CAN YOU HELP ME?

YES, MA'AM. I CAN HELP YOU. WHAT COULD I DO THAT WOULD MAKE YOU HAPPY? IS THERE, SAY, SOMETHING I COULD GIVE YOU THAT WOULD MAKE EVERYTHING BETTER?

OH, WHAT A NICE GIRL YOU ARE. THAT'S OKAY. I'LL GET MY NEIGHBOR TO HELP ME. HE'S YOUNG AND UNDERSTANDS WHAT MY MACHINES NEED FROM ME.

MA'AM, COULD YOU HOLD ON ONE SECOND?

LET GO OF ME, BEN.

IT'S JUST A BACKRUB, NORA.

I HEARD THINGS WERE OVER WITH THAT BEAR...

HI, MRS. NELSON? IS YOUR ADDRESS 5362 PERLITA? AND DO YOU PREFER LILIES OR ROSES?

I GET THE THINGS I WANT. I'M NOT GONNA QUIT, NORA.

TWEE ASS BABY

BEARS

WELL, I JUST DID. STAY AWAY FROM ME.

I GAVE HER ALL THE MONEY I HAD IN MY WALLET. $75. PLUS A DOZEN ROSES AND AN APOLOGY THAT PEOPLE CAN BE SUCH JERKS.

I ALSO HELPED HER WITH A LIGHTBULB THAT BLEW OUT. AND HELPED FINISH HER PUZZLE. AND FIND HER TV REMOTE.

...SHE WAS KINDA NEEDY.

EVERYTHING'S GREAT, MOM. I'M JUST BUSY.

GRAH.

SNAP

SNAP

SNAP

155

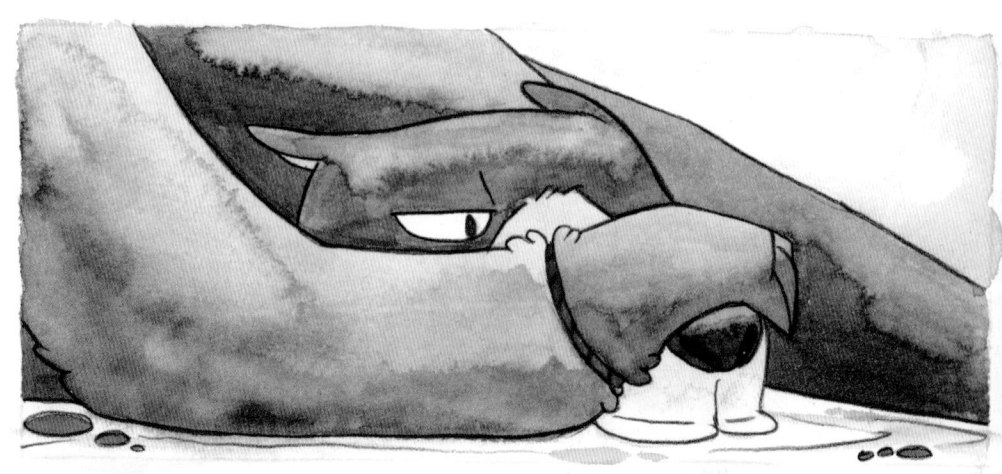

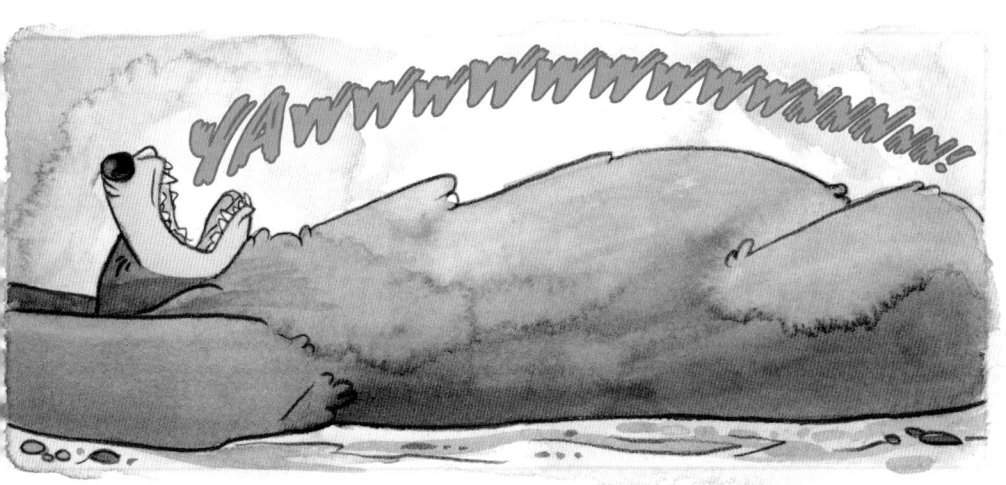

GRUMBLE

I KNOW THERE'S A CHANCE I'LL NEVER SEE THE BEAR AGAIN.

BUT WHAT WILL NEVER CHANGE IS HOW MUCH WE WERE IN LOVE.

Character Sketches

BEAR ///

NORA ♡ BEAR

NORA
(2ND)

♡ NORA

Cover Process

Thumbnail!

Inks!

Colors!

Logo!

Pamela Ribon co-created and currently writes the roller derby comic *SLAM!*, and has penned guest issues of *Rick and Morty*™. Her screenwriting work includes *Moana* and *Ralph Breaks the Internet: Wreck-It Ralph 2*. She's a best-selling author, frequent troublemaker, and true fan of you.

Cat Farris is a native Portlander, an artist, and is pretty sure she's just making this up as she goes along. She is supported in this venture by the world's most beautiful husband, the laziest greyhound, and an all-star cast of Helioscope studiomates.

Saida Temofonte is originally from Italy. She letters comics for DC Comics, Lion Forge, Kymera Press, Oni Press and IDW, and calls Los Angeles her beloved home now.

More Oni Press Books

you might enjoy...

A BOY AND A GIRL
By Jamie S. Rich
& Natalie Nourigat
ISBN 978-1-62010-089-9

**HOPELESS SAVAGES:
BREAK**
By Jen Van Meter,
Meredith McClaren,
and Christine Norrie
ISBN 978-1-62010-252-7

**KIM REAPER, VOL. 1:
GRIM BEGINNINGS**
By Sarah Graley
ISBN 978-1-62010-455-2

LUCKY PENNY
By Ananth Hirsh
& Yuko Ota
ISBN 978-1-62010-287-9

THE PEOPLE INSIDE
By Ray Fawkes
ISBN 978-1-62010-168-1

**SCOTT PILGRIM, VOL. 1:
PRECIOUS LITTLE LIFE**
By Bryan Lee O'Malley
ISBN 978-1-62010-000-4